D0264209

# ROBBiE
### and the
# RAAAH

# ROBBIE
## and the
# RAAAH

## STEVEN BUTLER
### Illustrated by Nigel Baines

### Orion
Children's Books

ORION CHILDREN'S BOOKS

First published in Great Britain in 2017
by Hodder and Stoughton

1 3 5 7 9 10 8 6 4 2

Text © Steven Butler 2017
Illustrations © Nigel Baines 2017

The moral rights of the author and illustrator have been asserted.

All rights reserved.
No part of this publication may be reproduced, stored in
a retrieval system, or transmitted, in any form or by any means, without
the prior permission in writing of the publisher, nor be otherwise circulated
in any form of binding or cover other than that in which it is published
and without a similar condition including this condition being
imposed on the subsequent purchaser.

A CIP catalogue record for this book
is available from the British Library.

ISBN 978 1 5101 0191 3

Printed and bound in China

The paper and board used in this book are
made from wood from responsible sources.

Orion Children's Books
An imprint of
Hachette Children's Group
Part of Hodder and Stoughton
Carmelite House
50 Victoria Embankment
London EC4Y 0DZ

An Hachette UK Company
www.hachette.co.uk

www.orionchildrensbooks.co.uk

*For Kirsten Grant, my fashion guru*
*and booky superhero*
*— S.B.*

# Contents

# Chapter One

Robbie looked up from his workbook and GROANED. The classroom was too hot, and the maths problems were too hard.

Robbie always behaved himself. He did his work exactly when he was told and he never complained … but today, something felt different.

Robbie pulled a face and was about to groan a REALLY big GROAN when something caught his eye.

In the bushes outside the classroom window, Robbie thought he saw something moving about.

Something huge.

Something HAIRY.

At lunchtime the dinner lady
served up cold mushy peas
and flabby pork. It looked
DISGUSTING!

Robbie was about to grumble,
when he thought he spotted a huge,
hairy shadow lurking near the
stock cupboards.

What was going on?

# Chapter Two

At 3 o'clock, **The R A A A H** was waiting for Robbie at the school gates.

The **RAAAH** was enormous and covered in bright orange hair with purple spots. Its claws were sharp, its teeth were pointy and its horns were twisty.

'Hello,' stammered Robbie.

'RAAAH!'

said **The RAAAH.**

Robbie ran home as fast as he could and **The R A A A H** thundered along close behind. It squashed cars flat and knocked over lamp posts. It kicked dustbins right across town and shattered windows with the loudness of its *RAAAH*-ing.

Robbie was terrified.

'Mum!' Robbie yelled, shoving open the front door and running into the living room.

'MUM! IT'S A MONSTER!'

The **RAAAH** was too big to use the front door so it burst through the living room wall.

Mum was on the sofa reading a book. She looked up at Robbie and **The RAAAH**, and smiled. 'Oh you found it,' she said.

Why wasn't Mum screaming and flapping around like a crazy rooster?

'MUM, IT'S A MONSTER!' Robbie shouted again. He pointed just to make sure Mum hadn't missed the massive beast.

Was he imagining it, or was
**The RAAAH** grinning and
wagging its tail?

Mum saw the horrified look on
Robbie's face and laughed. 'There's
nothing to worry about, Robbie.
You found your **RAAAH**... that's
all.'

'My what?'
asked Robbie.

'Your **RAAAH!**' said Mum. 'We all have a temper. Sometimes, when we get very fed up, it comes to visit. I have a **BLAAARG**.'

A hairy, yellow monster trotted
in from the kitchen and waved.
Robbie gasped and ducked behind
**The RAAAH**.

'What's that?' he whimpered.

'I just told you, darling,' Mum said.
'This is my **BLAAARG!**'

Mum always yelled '**BLAAARG**' when she was cross, Robbie thought.

**The BLAAARG** sat on the sofa next to Mum and handed her a biscuit.

'Haven't you ever noticed it before?' Mum asked.

Just then Dad walked in through
the back door.

'You found it,' he said.

'But Dad,' said Robbie.
'It's … it's …'

'It's your temper. A fine looking
**RAAAH**,' said Dad. 'I have a
**DUUUH**, myself.'

Dad's **DUUUH** ran in from the garden chewing on the shovel from the shed. It was tall and thin, and covered in scary-looking blue spikes.

Dad always yelled '**DUUUH**' when
he was cross, Robbie thought.

'Now that you've found it,' Dad said, 'you're allowed one whole day of *RAAAH*-ing before you have to put him away.'

'Put **The RAAAH** away?'

'Yes,' said Mum. 'We each get one day, and then we can only call our **RAAAHS** or **BLAAARGS** or **DUUUHS** out when they are extra-specially needed.'

Robbie looked up at **The RAAAH**.
**The RAAAH** looked down
at Robbie.

'It's too late today,' said Dad. 'You'll
have to take **The RAAAH** out
tomorrow.'

That night Robbie and 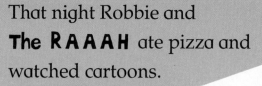 **The RAAAH** ate pizza and watched cartoons.

At bedtime **The RAAAH** couldn't fit into Robbie's bed, so it slept on the rug. Robbie slept on its belly, listening to the deep rumble of **The RAAAH'S** snoring.

# Chapter Three

'Today's the day,' Mum said, marching into Robbie's bedroom with a small bowl of breakfast for him, and a dustbin full of breakfast for **The R A A A H**. 'Off to school, you two.'

'Have fun *RAAAH*-ing,' said Dad.

**The RAAAH** swung Robbie onto its back and they galloped over the rooftops towards school.

Robbie felt a tingle of excitement
as they crashed through the classroom
door. Everyone screamed.

For the first time, Robbie noticed other people's tempers in the classroom. Terrance Phipps had a chubby, little **OOOW** under his desk, and Veronica Tanner's **WHAAAT** was snuggled on her shoulder.

'Today we're going to work on our spellings,' said Miss Grant. Robbie noticed a small, green monster twitching nervously on the bookshelf. It was Miss Grant's **HMMM**.

Spellings?

Robbie pulled a face at **The RAAAH**.

**The RAAAH** pulled a face at Robbie.

'RAAAAAAAAAAAAAAAHHH!'
they bellowed.

The walls shook, the lights flickered,
Miss Grant's glasses flew off and her
**HMMM** landed in the sink.

'I mean …' said Miss Grant, 'I mean
… let's paint the classroom walls!'
Everyone cheered. Robbie stood
on a chair and painted a picture
of **The RAAAH** as high as the
ceiling.

At lunch, the dinner lady said they were having boiled cabbage and liver.

Robbie stuck his tongue out at **The R A A A H**.

**The R A A A H** stuck its tongue out at Robbie.

'RAAAAAAAAAAAAAAAAHHH!'
they bellowed.

'I mean …' said the dinner lady,
hugging her **YUUUCK**. 'I mean …
CHICKEN NUGGET FOOD
FIGHT!'

It was BRILLIANT.

# Chapter 4

After school, **The RAAAH** taught Robbie the best spot for TANTRUMS in the aisle of the supermarket, and just the right howl to get an extra dollop of ice cream from Mr Swizzle's ice cream van!

Back at home, Robbie and **The RAAAH** sat on the roof until the moon was full and round in the night sky.

Robbie smiled at **The RAAAH**.

**The RAAAH** smiled at Robbie.

'Robbie,' Mum called up the chimney. 'That's your one day up. It's time to put the **RAAAH** away.'

'Control your temper, son,' yelled Dad.

The **RAAAH** swung Robbie onto its back and squeezed through the bedroom window.

'Goodnight,' said Robbie.

'RAAAH!' said **The RAAAH**,
and wriggled into the wardrobe.

Robbie climbed into bed and sat quietly in the dark for a moment.

When would he have the chance to *RAAAH* again?

What if he didn't get grumpy for ages?

Robbie hopped back out of bed
and tried a few stamps on the rug,
but he didn't feel angry. All the
*RAAAH*-ing had cheered him up.

He sneaked to the cupboard …

'**RAAAH?**' Robbie whispered.

Robbie pulled on the handle and opened the door …

The cupboard was empty.
The **RAAAH** was gone!